THE
EDINBURGH
MILITARY
JATTOO
1966

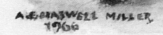

A. E. HASWELL MILLER
1966

PROGRAMME
1/-

The Massed Pipes and Drums march across the narrow
drawbridge of Edinburgh Castle and onto the Esplanade.

The Edinburgh Military Tattoo began its existence during the Edinburgh Festival of 1950.
It has since grown into a world renowned 1,000 strong cast spectacle. At the core of the
experience is the haunting sound of several hundred pipers and drummers performing on
the Esplanade of Edinburgh Castle. At the same time, the Tattoo has become famous for
presenting a versatile display of colour and culture created by groups of dedicated
performers who have been brought together from all corners of the world.

Let this book serve either as a lasting memory of an unforgettable experience or
as an enticing portfolio to encourage a visit to the Edinburgh Military Tattoo.

Graeme Wallace

The bonnet, medals and plaid brooch of a Scots Guard piper.

I would like to thank the organisers of The Edinburgh Military Tattoo for inviting me to publish a pictorial record of their event and providing me with the opportunity to produce this book. I have endeavoured to capture the event and its magnificent location on the Esplanade of Edinburgh Castle, perched up on its volcanic rock. I have also tried to portray the work that goes on behind the scenes and the scale of the production. Finally I wanted to capture the sense of feeling and emotion from the performers – the anticipation, the excitement and the satisfaction.

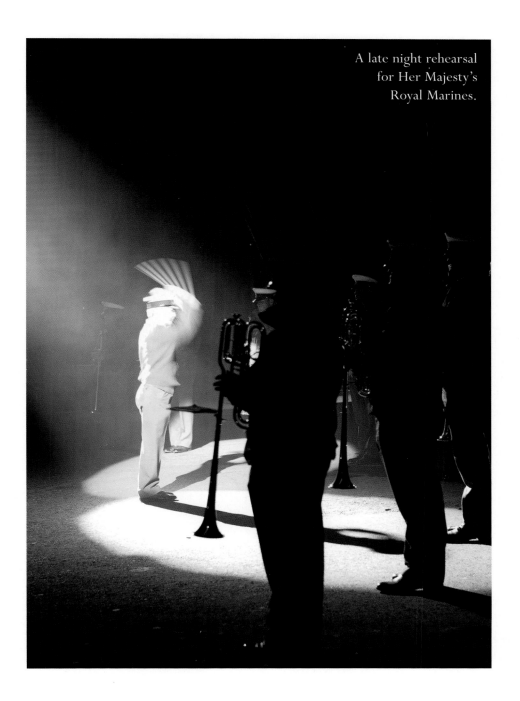

A late night rehearsal for Her Majesty's Royal Marines.

I would like to thank the performers for putting up with me as my camera lens zoomed in on them during their practices and performances and to the Drum and Pipe Majors for posing instead of taking a coffee break. I hope this book does the show and its performers proud and that it reveals a more personal side to the Tattoo.

Graeme Wallace

£1.00 from the sale of every book will be donated to the Army Benevolent Fund.

ACKNOWLEDGEMENTS

Photography by **Graeme Wallace**
except pages 5, 11, 12, 18, 19, 72-77 supplied by
The Edinburgh Military Tattoo
and page 13 © **The Scotsman Publications Ltd**

*Painting "Beating Retreat on the Esplanade" Edinburgh Castle
by* **Christopher Clark RI** *(1875-1942) reproduced by kind
permission of* **The Edinburgh Military Tattoo** *(page 10)*

Caricatures by **Douglas N. Anderson** *(pages 15-16)*

Text edited by **Roddy Martine**

Designed by **Melvin Creative**

Printed by **Printer Trento, Italy**

Published by **GW Publishing**,
*PO Box 6091, Thatcham, Berks, RG19 8XZ.
Tel + 44 (0)1635 268080*
www.gwpublishing.com

First Published 2006

FOREWORD

BUCKINGHAM PALACE

As Patron of The Edinburgh Military Tattoo, I am delighted to write the foreword to this new publication.

The magic of the Tattoo has enthralled millions of people from around the world for over 56 years, indeed, it has been sold out for the last eight. The Tattoo generates an estimated £87 million for the Scottish economy each August and has become a major contributor to Service charities and the Arts.

This volume captures the impressive scale of the production; it contains stunning photography of the event and those who perform in it. It is a magnificent record of this great Scottish Tattoo.

HRH Princess Anne, The Princess Royal.
Royal Patron – The Edinburgh Military Tattoo.

The Massed Pipes and Drums march through the castle gates and onto the Esplanade to begin the performance.

A working dress rehearsal of the
Massed Pipes and Drums under the
battlements of Edinburgh Castle.

CONTENTS

Edinburgh Castle.

THE CASTLE

It is easy to wax lyrical about Edinburgh Castle perched high upon its extinct volcanic rock. From its dominant position, this great fortress has witnessed many of the great events of Scotland's history. It is the symbolic heart of the Kingdom of Scots.

Once there were Iron-age forts on this site, but as Scotland began to evolve into a nation state during the latter part of the first millennium, the strategic location of Edinburgh's castle rock came into its own. With the Capital of Scotland then at Dunfermline, across the Firth of Forth, it was the Saxon Queen Margaret, wife of Malcolm III, who first used Edinburgh as a retreat in the 11th century. Following her death in 1093, her son, David I, built a small chapel in her memory, and this remains the oldest surviving structure to be seen within the castle walls.

Throughout five centuries of attack from invading English, Edinburgh Castle has remained defiant, despite being burned and battered during the Scottish Wars of Independence which lasted from 1296 until the mid-1540s. In 1359, David II introduced ambitious defence works, and in the following century the castle was used by James III as an ordinance factory. The Great Hall was added by his son, James IV, who so tragically died on the Battlefield of Flodden in 1513. Following the murder of her private secretary David Riccio, Mary Queen of Scots was persuaded to move into the royal lodging quarters where her son, the future James VI of Scotland, I of England, was born in 1566.

Repeatedly repaired and strengthened, Edinburgh Castle became an even more formidable fortress, resisting assaults from the Covenanters in 1640, holding out for James VIII and II in 1688 and for George II in 1745 during the Jacobite Uprising. Bonnie Prince Charlie's unsuccessful attempt to capture it that year was the final siege of its long history. From time to time it was starved into submission, or betrayed from within, but only twice did Edinburgh Castle fall to its attackers in combat. On both occasions, it was to the Scots who were reclaiming it back from the English.

In 1773, work began on the ceremonial parade ground in front of the castle entrance, the Esplanade upon which the Edinburgh Military Tattoo now takes place. Approximately sixty years later, this expanse was broadened and landscaped with the introduction of walls and railings.

This development, however, signalled that the castle's principal role as a fortress stronghold had come to an end. After the 1745 Jacobite Uprising, it was principally used as a barracks, and during the Napoleonic Wars of the 18th century, served as a grim, but effective prison for French prisoners-of-war.

Today, it provides the safe for some of Scotland's greatest treasures; not least the Stone of Destiny upon which all British monarchs are crowned. In the Crown Room are housed the Honours of Scotland – the Scottish Crown, believed to be the oldest in Europe; the Sceptre, a gift to James IV from Pope Alexander VI in 1494, and the Sword of State, a gift to that same King from Pope Julius II.

Edinburgh Castle remains the headquarters of the 52 Infantry Brigade of the British Army, and houses several regimental headquarters. The National War Museum of Scotland is housed in two sites. The first is located in the Hospital block; the second in the Queen Anne Barracks. Exhibitions relate to Scotland's three armed services. The Scottish National War Memorial is next door to the Queen Anne Barracks, and contains the names of the dead from two world wars and conflicts since.

Edinburgh Castle has become Britain's second most popular tourist attraction, annually receiving in the region of one million visitors. Standing sentinel over Scotland's 21st century Capital, it is a constant reminder of a thousand years of history, a living reflection of a tumultuous and noble past.

A BRIEF HISTORY

The 1st Duke of Marlborough's triumphant wars in the Low Countries at the start of the 18th century seem long ago and far away. Yet it is in those wars that we find the origin of the word Tattoo. The Dutch taverns which the British soldiers frequented would close to the cry of " Doe den tap toe" meaning literally "Turn off the taps", and consequently "tap toe" became a drum and bugle signal which summoned the soldiery back to their quarters for the night. The "tap toe" gradually evolved into a ritual to formally mark the end of a day, not unlike the ceremony of "Beating the Retreat."

Later, in Russia, devout soldiers added a hymn of thanksgiving for their having lived another day. The habit spread across Europe until, by the beginning of the last century, the British had joined the Germans, Austrians and French in developing an event called a Tattoo, combining spectacle with martial and religious music. It rapidly became less of a military pageant and more a public performance.

And what a public performance the Edinburgh Military Tattoo has become! The Massed Pipes and Drums, the Military Bands, the thrill of the action, the precision of the drill, the splendour of the setting, and the richness of the uniforms; all combine to make this a truly magical experience.

The Edinburgh Military Tattoo, however, began as a series of evening displays of piping and dancing on the Castle Esplanade. So successful were these shows, and so large the crowds which they attracted, that in 1949, Scottish Command and Edinburgh Town Council (as the City of Edinburgh Council was then known), agreed to co-operate in presenting a full Military Tattoo as the Army in Scotland's contribution to the Edinburgh International Festival, then in its fourth year. It has been an annual event on the Castle Esplanade ever since.

Beating the retreat on the Esplanade of
Edinburgh Castle by Christopher Clark RI (1875-1942).

More than eleven million people have been to see it, some two hundred thousand each year. Another one hundred million enjoy the spectacle regularly on world-wide television. Its reputation is so great and demand for tickets so high that over fifty per cent of the tickets are sold within the first two weeks of their going on sale.

With its unique blend of music, pageantry, action and theatre, all sensationally enhanced by the backdrop of Edinburgh Castle, the Edinburgh Military Tattoo is beyond doubt one of the greatest shows on earth. Once seen, it is never forgotten.

Black and white images of the 1952 Tattoo (above) and 1973 Tattoo (below) prior to the introduction of a modular stadium.

A Lone Piper on the Battlements of Edinburgh Castle painted by Lieutenant Colonel Olaf MacLeod in 1981.

The Edinburgh Military Tattoo has been a sell-out for the past eight years. It annually entertains an audience of 220,000 during the month of August. The Edinburgh Military Tattoo of 2005, at which the majority of the photographs in the book were taken, had a cast of 1,000 including performers representing all of the Scottish Infantry Regiments; three Pipes and Bands from the Commonwealth, and the Pipes and Bands of four University Officer Training Corps - a record of 13 Pipes & Drums.

Fast moving, all action, precision riding was demonstrated by the remarkable Imps Motorcycle Team. The 38 young riders make this the largest motorcycle display group in the world and more than 1,000 young people can proudly call themselves Ex Imps. The Imps themselves are aged between five and sixteen, many of them veterans of prime time television. From the sound of revving engines to the awe of a billowing fire jump and the suspense of a combination 'cross-over' routine, the young riders provided a breathtaking display of skill and precision.

Formed in June 1995, The Trinidad and Tobago Defence Force Steel Orchestra, the only marching military steel orchestra in the world was another triumph. Their heady mix of soul and calypso has seen the band compete in numerous competitions, winning titles for both pan and calypso. The Russian Cossack State Dance Company comprising 40 dancers, musicians and singers brought with it a breathtaking dynamism. Cossacks are a vital part of Russian cultural and military heritage.

The New Zealand Highland Dancers from Wellington performed at the Queen's Golden Jubilee Tattoo in 2002. For the 2005 show, a specially devised dance was created to reflect the Tattoo's Royal Navy theme. Under the direction of former World Highland Dancing Champion Billy Forsyth, assisted by New Zealand Dance Band Director, Shirley Anne Thompson, the 100-strong dance troupe varied in age from teenagers through to their early twenties, and many have been dancing since they were four years old.

The Guard of His Majesty The King of Norway's Band and Drill Team were also no strangers to the Edinburgh Tattoo, having first taken part in 1961. These guardsmen are all undergoing compulsory military service for twelve months and are, on average, between 19 and 20 years old. The company on this occasion had also taken part in the Edinburgh Military Tattoo's performance in Australia.

The Kevock Choir (The Tattoo Choir), conducted by Graham Lovett, is recognised as one of Scotland's foremost large choirs. Founded in 1967 by former pupils of Lasswade High School in Edinburgh, it is named after the adjacent Kevock Valley, and has become a mainstay of Tattoo performances.

An acknowledgement should also be given to the Army School of Piping, which has its headquarters in Edinburgh. The school was founded in 1910 on the initiative of the Piobaireachd Society, and among its regular courses are a seven month Pipe Major's Course, and a three-week Class One Pipers' Course. The school has historically been responsible for putting together the programme of pipe music at the Tattoo.

The Edinburgh Military Tattoo is registered as a non-profit making charity and its proceeds are annually donated to Service charities and the Arts.

Her Majesty Queen Elizabeth and Prince Philip arrive at Edinburgh Castle for the Golden Jubilee performance in 2002.

TATTOO PRODUCERS

Lieutenant Colonel George Malcolm (1950-51)
The hereditary Chief of Clan Malcolm, Lt. Col. George Malcolm was a commander of the 8th Battalion, The Argyll and Sutherland Highlanders seeing action during the First World War. In 1949 he produced 'The King's Men', a display at Edinburgh Castle which included Changing of the Guards by the 9th Lancers and the Scots Guards, as well as a selection of musical items. This was the show which evolved in to the first full Edinburgh Military Tattoo in 1950. With over 100,000 seeing the three week show including H. M. Queen Elizabeth and Princess Margaret, it proved that Scotland could host an outdoor performance and was the beginning of many great events to follow.

Brigadier Lieutenant Colonel Alasdair Maclean, CBE (1953-66)
Thirty-three years a soldier, serving in the Queen's Own Cameron Highlanders Lt. Col. Alasdair Maclean commanded the 1st Cameron Highlanders during the Second World War. Having been Director of the Tattoo since 1950 he took over as Producer in 1953. He was particularly influential in gaining international recognition for the Tattoo and establishing it as a most significant attraction by taking the show overseas. In 1955 he took the Edinburgh Tattoo in its entirety to Copenhagan and in 1964 he took with him to Australia the pipes and drums of the three Scottish regiments to perform in the Sydney Searchlight Tattoo.

Brigadier Jack Sanderson, DSO, OBE (1967-75)
A former Scots Guard, Brigadier Jack Sanderson had a distinguished military career seeing active service during the Second World War. He was appointed Brigadier, Highland District then Commander, Edinburgh Area toward the end of his military career. Raising the profile of the Tattoo still further, it was filmed for the first time in colour for the TV in 1968. Toward the end of Sanderson's tenure the old fashioned scaffolding stands and bench seating was finally replaced by the sophisticated modular steel tubular structure still in use today, a vast improvement adding a further degree of professionalism to the event.

Lieutenant Colonel Leslie Dow, OBE (1976-1991)
The last Commanding Officer of the 1st Battalion, The Cameronians (Scottish Rifles) Lt. Col. Leslie Dow's regiment was involved in the Aden Campaign during which time it acquitted itself with distinction. With the regiment being disbanded in 1968 Dow took personal responsibility, producing the final parade, a moving and stirring event for all those present. The longest serving producer his creative thinking and daring deeds led to his taking part in a Motorcycle display, but no he was not riding, he lay down on the ground allowing the motorcyclists to leap over him. In 1980 The Royal Band of H.M. The Sultan of Oman performed at the Tattoo, their first ever performance outside the Gulf States.

Major Sir Michael Parker, CVO, MBE (1992-1994)
Major Michael Parker produced his first Tattoo almost by accident, as a Second Lieutenant in the Queen's Own Hussars in 1965. He went on to oversee the musical fireworks for the wedding of Their Royal Highnesses the Prince and Princess of Wales, the national tribute on London's Horse Guard Parade to mark the ninetieth birthday of H.M. Queen Elizabeth the Queen Mother and the autumn celebrations commemorating the fortieth anniversary of the accession to the throne of H.M. Queen Elizabeth II. This history lead to Major Parker introducing a more flamboyant and theatrical style when he became Producer in 1992. Producing stirring, patriotic shows his performances were themed around Macbeth, Mary Queen of Scots and King James VI. His final show in 1994 paid tribute to the disbandenement of the Gordon Highlanders. In 2002, Sir Michael was the mastermind behind Her Majesty the Queen's Golden Jubilee celebrations in London.

Brigadier Melville Jameson, CBE, DL (1995 – present)

Brigadier Melville Jameson was commissioned into the Royal Scots Greys (which in 1971 amalgamated with the 3rd Carabiniers to form the Royal Scots Dragoon Guards) and subsequently spent three years as a squadron leader in Chieftain tanks among other duties before being appointed to command the regiment in 1986. He was later appointed Colonel on the Military Secretary's Staff, then Commander, 51st Highland Brigade before taking early retirement in 1996 to concentrate on the Tattoo.

Far from sitting back and maintaining the established annual performance, Brigadier Jameson has improved the Tattoo year on year with a cast selected from a versatile range of performers recruited from around the globe. Each year Jameson travels the world seeking out those unique acts which express nationality and culture and which will enhance the Tattoo's diversity. "It is uncommon for those acts which approach us directly to fit the bill," he says. "I am looking for the finest performances that are fresh and new and will thrill our audience."

Furthermore, he believes that music is paramount to the success of each show, particularly in the Finale with Bands and Pipes and Drums - "Combined Music." To achieve this, he personally selects the music in consultation with the Senior Director of Music and the Director of Army Bagpipe Music. "It must leave the audience feeling proud, emotional, and even patriotic!"

In 1997, The Trinidad and Tobago Defence Force Steel Band and Drums played Caribbean calypsos. 1998 saw the Central Band of the Russian Navy which was the first ever performance by Russian nationals, and the Caribbean was represented again by the Barbados Defence Force Band in 1999. This international contribution ensures that there will be at least one surprise every year.

The Brigadier states that the overall performance is built around four pillars; these are 1) The Massed Pipes and Drums, 2) The Massed Military Bands, 3) Variety Acts from home and abroad, and 4) The Finale. However, he is quick to recognise a 5th pillar, namely the production crew headed up by Production Manager, Steve Walsh, MBE, ex-Gordon Highlander!

Although Brigadier Jameson's shows are predominantly musical, he always tries to ensure some action for the younger members of the audience; these acts, of course, bring with them the greatest risks of the unexpected!

In 2000, for the first time, the Edinburgh Tattoo went overseas to Wellington, New Zealand. A full size-replica backdrop of Edinburgh Castle was erected and a cast recruited from UK and New Zealand forces performed four shows to 20,000 spectators per night during the New Zealand Arts Festival.

In 2005, the Tattoo was invited to visit Australia, where it performed to full houses on six nights in the Aussie Stadium, Sydney. The Show was titled "Salute to Australia," and was seen by a total audience of 160,000.

That same year, with a cast of 1,000 performers, including the Massed Pipes and Drums of seven of the eight Scottish Regiments, images were projected on the walls of Edinburgh Castle for the first time; these new backdrops not only support the performers, but also help to convey the theme and message of the event, bringing the very latest technology to the ancient fortress.

Brigadier Melville Jameson in conversation with Senior Pipe Major Sellwood of The Scots Guards.

The Royal Scots Dragoon Guards (Carabiniers and Greys)

The Royal Scots Dragoon Guards is Scotland's senior Regiment and the only regular cavalry. Formed on the orders of King Charles II in 1678, the Regiment has a record 327 years of distinguished service to the Crown.

The Royal Scots (The Royal Regiment)

The Royal Scots were formed in 1633 when Sir John Hepburn under a Royal Warrant granted by King Charles I, raised a body of men in Scotland for service in France. They are the oldest Infantry Regiment, and also known as "First of Foot, right of the line and the pride of the British Army."

The King's Own Scottish Borderers

Raised in 1689 in Edinburgh by David Leslie, the third Earl of Leven to protect the Scottish Capital against attacks from the forces loyal to the deposed King James. During 316 years of services to the Crown, the Regiment has been awarded six Victoria Crosses for Bravery, one of which was awarded to Piper Daniel Laidlaw at the Battle of Loos in 1915

The Highlanders (Seaforth, Gordons and Camerons)

The Highlanders was established in 1994 with the amalgamation of The Gordon Highlanders raised in 1794 and The Queen's Own Highlanders which itself was an amalgamation formed in 1961 of The Seaforth Highlanders and The Queen's Own Cameron Highlanders. The Duke of Gordon was assisted by his wife, the Duchess Jean in recruiting the original Gordon Highlanders by riding to country fairs in highland bonnet and regimental jacket; giving a kiss along with a shilling to the men she enlisted.

Scots Guards

In the autumn of 1641 Ireland rose in rebellion against the Scottish settlers colonizing Ulster. As a result, King Charles I sanctioned the raising of Scottish regiments for service in Ireland and it is here that the history of the Scots Guards began.

The Royal Highland Fusiliers (Princess Margaret's Own Glasgow & Ayrshire Regiment)

The Royal Highland Fusiliers were formed in 1959 by the amalgamation of the Royal Scots Fusiliers and the Highland Light Infantry, raised respectively in 1678 and 1777. In honour of both Regiments they still wear the Highland Light Infantry's Mackenzie tartan trews (trousers) and the Flaming Grenade cap badge from the Royal Scots Fusiliers.

The Black Watch (Royal Highland Regiment)

The Black Watch was raised in 1739 near Aberfeldy in Perthshire to help police the Highlands in the wake of the Jacobite rebellion. Derived from the Gaelic nickname 'An Freiceadan Dubh', The Black Watch title reflects the dark colour of their tartan and the original role the Regiment performed 'watching' the Highlands.

The Argyll and Sutherland Highlanders (Princess Louise's)

1881 saw the wholesale reorganisation of the British Army which brought into existence Princess Louise's Argyll and Sutherland Highlanders; an amalgamation of the old 91st Argyllshire Highlanders with the 93rd Sutherland Highlanders, famous for their heroic exploits at Balaklava.

THE SCOTTISH REGIMENTS AND A BRIEF HISTORY OF SCOTLAND

Much of Scotland's history is preoccupied with internal clan and family feuds, religious dispute, or keeping the enemy at bay. As a result, the Scots have developed a reputation for being fearless fighting men. It is not so surprising, therefore, that the Scottish Regiments emerged from this tradition.

The first acknowledged King of Scotland was Kenneth MacAlpin, who in 843 united the West Coast Scots with the largely East Coast Picts to fight against invading Vikings from Denmark.

By 1059, the warring factions had largely been brought together under Malcolm III (Canmore) who, having disposed of his cousin MacBeth, married the Saxon Princess Margaret Atheling, and ruled Scotland for thirty five years. To guarantee the peace with their southern neighbours, at least in the short term, their daughter Maud was married to Henry I of England.

In 1286, Malcolm's great-great-great grandson Alexander III fell from a horse and was killed. The heir to the Scottish throne was his 3-year old granddaughter who was living in Norway. The small princess died on her way to Scotland, and Edward I of England immediately appointed himself over-lord of Scotland. It was the beginning of the Scottish Wars of Independence which would drag on for over two and a half centuries.

Essential to Scotland's story at this stage was the emergence of Robert the Bruce, who, after much adversity, won a great victory against Edward I's son and the English army at Bannockburn in 1314. King Robert Bruce's daughter Marjory married Walter, Steward of Scotland in 1371 and founded Scotland's Royal Stewart dynasty.

However, despite their being proven monarchs of all Scotland, many of the Highland, and certain Lowland, clan chiefs opposed the Stewarts. The Battle of Harlaw in 1411 brought matters to a head and diminished the power of the West Coast Clan Donald and its followers.

In 1503, the marriage of James IV to Margaret Tudor, the sister of England's Henry VIII, should have guaranteed peace thereafter, but alas, in 1512, England attacked France. James had previously forged an alliance with the French king, and the Scottish army was decimated in the subsequent altercation fought on Flodden Moor, in England.

Scotland's next period of turbulence took place during the reign of James IV's granddaughter Mary Queen of Scots.

The Reformation was underway throughout Europe, and Scotland had, in her absence, adopted the Protestant religion. Having been married to the Dauphin of France, and briefly been Queen of France, the Catholic Mary returned to Scotland at the age of 19 to find herself challenged by the Protestant reformer John Knox. Surrounded by intrigue, she managed to hold on to power for six years before being driven into exile in England. Her baby son James VI was crowned at the Church of the Holy Rude in Stirling at such a young age that he would barely have known what was going on.

Following the death of his cousin, Queen Elizabeth I of England, in 1603, however, James VI of Scotland became James I of England uniting the crowns of the two countries. During his subsequent reign, and those of his son Charles I, and grandsons Charles II and James VIII and I, further violent splits occurred between the adherents of the old Catholic religion, and the emergent Protestantism. It was Charles I who raised The Royal Scots in 1633 and the Scots Guards in 1642, as his Royal Guard. The Royal Scots Fusiliers, which later became The Royal Highland Fusiliers, was raised in 1678 by the 5th Earl of Mar during the reign of Charles II.

In 1678, Charles II was also responsible for establishing the troop of Dragoons which three centuries later became known as The Royal Scots Dragoon Guards. In 1689, William of Orange, nephew and son-in-law of James VIII and III, seized the British throne to prevent James's son, by his second marriage from becoming king. James's supporters would thereafter be known as "Jacobites." William immediately created The Edinburgh Regiment, which eventually became The King's Own Scottish Borderers, tasked with protecting the Scottish Capital against the Jacobite threat.

The insurgency continued however, with James's son, also James, and his grandson, Bonnie Prince Charlie leading uprisings in the Highlands in 1715 and in 1745 but ending with Bonnie Prince Charlie's defeat at the Battle of Culloden in 1746. It was during this period that The 42nd Royal Highland Regiment was formed to police the Highlands. It later became know as The Black Watch.

Although no more battles were fought on Scottish soil after Culloden, the Scots continued to play an important part in Britain's ongoing military campaigns. The Argyll and Sutherland Highlanders and The Highlanders date from 1778, formed in the run up to the Napoleonic Wars in Europe. Since then Scottish regiments have played a significant part in every major conflict in which the United Kingdom has become involved.

The Royal Scots Dragoon Guards

In 1678, three independent troops of Dragoons were raised by order of King Charles II to counter the growing threat from the Covenanters; the Presbyterian movement which opposed the monarch's attempts to control the church. By 1681, additional troops had been raised and were brought together as the Royal Regiment of Dragoons. They were also unofficially known as the Scots Greys and Grey Dragoons as a result of being mounted on grey horses and wearing grey uniforms. Only the regimental pipers wore tartan, which was the Royal Stewart. In 1971, they amalgamated with the 3rd Carabiniers, Prince of Wales's Dragoon Guards to form the Royal Scots Dragoon Guards. The pipers continue to wear kilts of the Royal Stewart tartan.

Drum Major Orr of The Royal Scots Dragoon Guards (Carabiniers and Greys) with Lance Corporal Harnetty, Regimental Kettle Drummer, mounted on the Drum Horse and carrying the Regimental Standard which were presented to the Regiment by HM the Queen.

Immortalised in history for their charge at the Battle of Waterloo, The Royal Scots Dragoon Guards is the Senior Regiment and Scotland's only regular cavalry regiment. Horses were replaced by armoured vehicles in 1941. The Regiment is nevertheless still encouraged to maintain its equestrian association through regular participation in sporting events and competitions.

Pipe Major Potter of The Royal Scots Dragoon Guards (Carabiniers and Greys).

1st Battalion Scots Guards

Dating from 1642, The Scots Guards was formed to be the Royal Guard of King Charles I. The Regiment has had pipers from the very outset, but they were originally employed at the expense of the officers. It was not until 1856 that six pipers, including a pipe major, became official members of the Regiment having proven their importance during the Crimean War. Since then, pipers have been deployed with their Battalions on all overseas assignments. During the First World War, they would play their companies 'over the top' but this practice was stopped in 1915 after the loss of seven pipers and several others that were wounded. The pipers wear the Royal Stewart tartan.

Pipe Major Mackenzie of
1st Battalion The Scots Guards.

1st Battalion The Royal Scots (The Royal Regiment)

The oldest Infantry Regiment of the Line in the British Army, raised in 1633 for service in France. By 1635, the force had grown to over 8,000 including many who fought as mercenaries in the 'Green Brigade'. The Regiment has served the Crown without interruption ever since. The Royal Scots are renowned for their specialist roles in jungle and mountain warfare. Drum majors wear Hunting Stewart trews (the regimental tartan) while pipe majors wear the Sovereign's personal tartan, the Royal Stewart, an honour granted to them by King George V in 1933. Both tartans are displayed on the pipes drone cords.

Drum Major Hay and Pipe Major
Boyd of 1st Battalion The Royal
Scots (The Royal Regiment).

The 1st Battalion The Royal Highland Fusiliers (Princess Margaret's Own Glasgow and Ayrshire Regiment)

Formed in 1959 by the amalgamation of The Royal Scots Fusiliers (established 1678) and The Highland Light Infantry (established 1777). The Royal Scots Fusiliers was raised to deal with the religious upheaval in Scotland. The title Fusilier derives from the term used to describe soldiers using 'flintlock' muskets known as 'Fusils' while the 'Royal' status was gained in 1712 having completed a 10 year campaign under the Duke of Marlborough during which time they never lost a battle.

The Highland Light Infantry date back to 1777 as The 73rd Highlanders. Raised by John MacKenzie as the first clan regiment to counter the American War of Independence. The Drum Major still wears the MacKenzie tartan trews of the Highland Light Infantry while the rest of the band wear the Erskine tartan of the Royal Scots Fusiliers.

Drum Major MacDougall and Pipe Major Hall of 1st Battalion The Royal Highland Fusiliers (Princess Margaret's Own Glasgow and Ayrshire Regiment).

The 1st Battalion The King's Own Scottish Borderers

Originally named The Edinburgh Regiment, it was formed in 1689 within just two hours in order to protect the Scottish Capital against attacks from the Jacobite supporters of King James VII and II. The regiment first saw action at the Battle of Killiecrankie in July of that year, and is the only Scottish regiment to have taken part in all three of the decisive battles fought against Jacobite forces. Since then, the Regiment has fought in every major campaign that the British Army has undertaken. The name was changed to The King's Own Scottish Borderers in 1805.

In addition to playing music, the Pipe Band acts as the Regiment's Machine Gun Platoon. The drummers wear trews of the Leslie tartan, while the pipers wear the kilt of the Royal Stewart tartan. Both tartans are incorporated into the pipes drone cord.

Pipe Major Bell and
Drum Major Meikle
of 1st Battalion
The King's Own
Scottish Borderers.

The 1st Battalion The Black Watch (Royal Highland Regiment)

The Black Watch Regiment was formed in 1739 with the bringing together of ten companies of men (six of these having been established fourteen years earlier). These "trustworthy" Highlanders came from clans loyal to King George I and were responsible for enforcing the Law and keeping peace in the north of Scotland during the troubled times between, and immediately following, the Jacobite Risings. The name Black Watch arose from the Regiment's dark tartan and the "watch" they kept over the Highlands.

Pipers have been associated with the Regiment as far back as 1768 and a Black Watch band was in existence as early as 1773. The Black Watch pipers and drummers are first soldiers and musicians thereafter. Their historic contribution as soldiers on the field of battle has been impressive. The drummers wear the Black Watch tartan kilts while the pipers wear kilts of the Royal Stewart tartan. The pipe drones are adjoined with ribbons from both tartans.

Pipe Major Taylor and Drum Major Robson of 1st Battalion The Black Watch (Royal Highland Regiment).

1st Battalion The Argyll & Sutherland Highlanders
(Princess Louise's)

Formed in 1881 by the amalgamation of the 91st Argyllshire Highlanders with the 93rd Sutherland Highlanders. The Argyllshire Highlanders was originally formed in 1794 when Britain was at war with France. Five years later, in 1799, The Sutherland Highlanders was formed as a test of feudal duty from the able-bodied sons of tenants on the Sutherland estates in the North of Scotland. Their kilts were of the Sutherland tartan.

During the Crimean War, they became famous for the formation of the 'Thin Red Line' which repelled a charge of Russian cavalry on the morning of the Battle of Balaclava. Pipers and Drummers wear the Regimental Tartan.

Pipe Major Huxter and Drum Major Smith of 1st Battalion
The Argyll and Sutherland Highlanders (Princess Louise's).

The 1st Battalion The Highlanders (Seaforth, Gordons and Camerons)

The Seaforth Highlanders was raised by the Earl of Seaforth in 1778, and their first task was to defend the Channel Islands against attack from the French. The Cameron Highlanders was established several years later in 1793, and it too was tasked with supporting the war against France. The pipers and bandsmen wore the Cameron of Erracht tartan kilt in recognition of the Cameron Highlanders, and trews of the Mackenzie tartan in recognition of the Seaforth Highlanders.

The Gordon Highlanders was raised in 1794 by the 4th Duke of Gordon, and naturally wore the Gordon tartan kilt. With an equally exemplary history, they were amalgamated with the Queen's Own Highlanders in 1994 to form The Highlanders.

All three tartans deriving from these distinguished Highland regiments are today worn with pride. Both pipers and drummers wear the Cameron of Erracht kilt, while the remainder of the Regiment wear the Gordon kilt. All ranks also wear trews of the Mackenzie of Seaforth tartan. The cords of the pipe drones are Mackenzie, while the official tartan for the pipes is Gordon.

Drum Major Caldwell
and Pipe Major Mackenzie
of 1st Battalion The
Highlanders (Seaforth,
Gordons and Camerons).

Men of Valour

The members of the Pipes and Drums are all fighting servicemen for whom combat must take priority over their music. For example, the pipers and drummers of The Highlanders are all fully trained members of the Assault Pioneer Platoon, while The King's Own Scottish Borderers has the official role of Battalion Machine Gun Platoon. Pipe Band members of The Royal Scots Dragoon Guards have the dual role of also being tank crew men.

The image of pipers standing proud, playing their instruments and stirring their fellow soldiers into action in the face of their enemy is not exaggerated. In fact, many pipers have done just that, six of whom received the Victoria Cross for their bravery on the battlefield.

Piper George Findlater of The Gordon Highlanders won the award in Northwest India in 1897 for continuing to play his pipes despite one of his fellow pipers being shot in the chest and while he himself was shot in the ankles. Of the five pipers who led the charge, only one, Piper Kidd, made it to the Heights. Piper Findlater commented afterwards, "I remember the Colonel addressing the Regiment and the order Pipers to the Front!"

Piper Daniel Laidlaw of The King's Own Scottish Borderers also gained the medal for his bravery during the Battle of Loos in 1915. His battalion was advancing under heavy artillery fire and poisonous gas, suffering many casualties in the process. Piper Laidlaw played the Regimental March 'Blue Bonnets O'er the Border' as he marched along the trench parapet encouraging the advancing troops in defiance of the danger to his own life. He even continued to play when shot in the leg, and it was for this act of extreme bravery that he was awarded his Victoria Cross.

In 1916, Piper James Richardson of the Seaforth Highlanders of Canada was just twenty years old when he similarly played his pipes along the trenches during the First World War. Having successfully rallied the troops, he broke off to help save a fellow soldier and was killed as he returned to retrieve his pipes.

Pipe Major Bell of 1st Battalion
The King's Own Scottish Borderers.

REHEARSAL

The parade ground at Redford Cavalry Barracks in Edinburgh's south-western suburbs is the venue for the Tattoo's initial rehearsals. Some of the individual acts are already well practised, but only now will the production team be in a position to establish whether or not anything is amiss with the overall design of the show.

Painted onto the tarmac is a full size plan of the Castle Esplanade, complete to the last detail. The 'replica' esplanade at Redford Barracks is mapped out 70 metres and 25 metres, wider at the top than at the bottom, with the main entrance (the Castle Drawbridge) distinctly off-centre, adding further complexity to all of the formations.

So professional is the performance that one can scarcely credit the Army's Director of Bagpipe Music when he says, "We knock this show together in about three hours." The music is sent to all the bands that are scheduled to participate – military, civilian and overseas contributors – some six months in advance so that they all know the tunes thoroughly. When the bands meet for the

first time, less than a week before the show opens, it is necessary only to demonstrate that they have done their homework. This job, known as 'proving the music' involves playing through all the tunes. The Director can immediately gauge the feel of the music and the bands; he knows at once if the musicians have mastered their brief. Almost invariably they have, leaving him with the task of choreographing the ten minute performance.

The bands rehearse their marching and massed formations without playing so that everyone is confident about the various manoeuvres. It is not uncommon to complete the first rehearsal within three hours – and that includes a coffee break!

Thereafter, it is a matter of ensuring that it all runs smoothly. Army bands, of course, are groomed from the start to parade; civilian bands are not always used to parading en masse, nor to striding out in the march or marking time in a military fashion. However, despite the limited time, by dint of hard work and professionalism, the massed pipes and drums are ready for their display and the finale within four days.

The drill team of His Majesty the King of Norway's Guards practice on the parade ground of Redford Barracks, on the outskirts of Edinburgh.

The only thing that cannot be replicated at the Redford Barracks parade ground is the unforgiving slope on the Esplanade of Edinburgh Castle. The fourteen foot drop gives parading and performing on the Esplanade a different perspective.

Now is the time to sharpen up the action, give the drill a final polish and perfect the dressing. Here the Production Manager comes to the fore; he is responsible for marshalling all of the Tattoo's cast on the Esplanade and for ensuring that everything flows smoothly under the spotlights and behind the scenes.

The Royal Marine Commandos abseil down the castle wall…

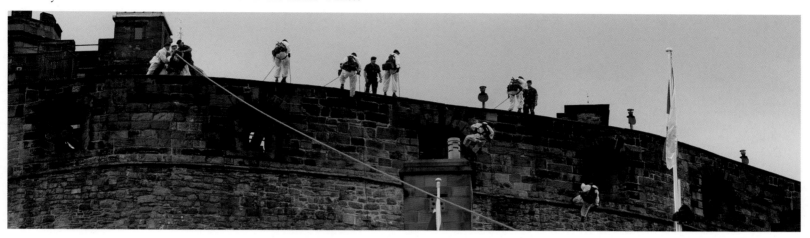

…The Imps Motor Cycle Team work on their Pyramid…

…and The King's Guard prepare for one last rehearsal.

A Trumpeter of His Majesty The King of Norway's Guard in rehearsal.

The swirl of a skirt worn by a member of the Russian Cossack State Dance Company.

Pipers of the South African Irish Regiment.

The performers have two rehearsals at the castle the day before the dress rehearsal - some in their costumes, most in civilian clothes, drab khaki or camouflage denim, perhaps with the odd splash of tartan — 'working dress.'

A piper of The 1st Battalion Scots Guards during rehearsal.

The Pipes and Drums of 1st Battalion The Argyll and Sutherland Highlanders (Princess Louise's).

A dancer from the Russian Cossack State Dance Company.

Limbo dancing to the music of the
Trinidad and Tobago Defence Force
Steel Orchestra.

Drummers of the band of Her Majesty's Royal Marines.

A musician with the Guard of His
Majesty The King of Norway's Band.

A "Double Jimmy" from the younger
members of The Imps Motorcycle team.

Bass Drummers of Her Majesty's Royal Marines.

A commando-style demonstration by
Her Majesty's Royal Marines.

Steel drums of The Trinidad and Tobago
Defence Force Steel Orchestra.

THE INSTRUMENTS
Bagpipes

Not all the pipers, incidentally, use identical instruments. There are standard Army bagpipes on issue, produced by some of the world's finest manufacturers. However, like many good things the pipes mature with age so although outstanding instruments are still being made, old pipes are often better than new. Many pipers therefore prefer to play their own rather than Army issue bagpipes; indeed they are encouraged to do so by the military authorities and take great pride in old sets of bagpipes, often elaborately decorated with ivory and silver, which can be worth several thousand pounds.

Drums of Her Majesty's Royal Marines.

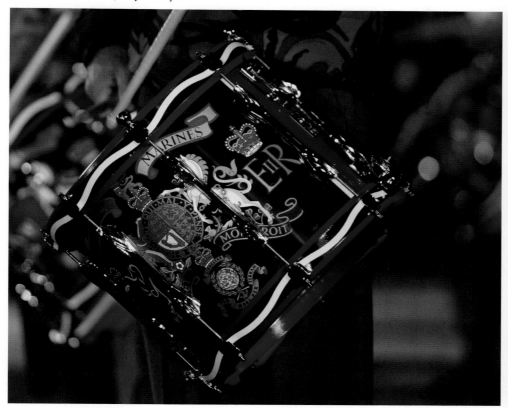

Drums of the 1st Battalion Irish Guards.

Drums of the 1st Battalion The Argyll and
Sutherland Highlanders (Princess Louise's).

Drums of the 1st Battalion The
King's Own Scottish Borderers.

Drums

The drum was the normal method of giving signals
on the battlefield or in camp. The drummer's
rhythm would advertise the changing watches or
beat the men to quarter as long ago as the days of
Drake and Hawkins.

Herald Trumpet.

Brass instruments, along with woodwind, are the main instruments of military bands.

Trombone (above) and Saxophone (below)

PLAYING IN

Before every performance the pipers play through all their tunes within the Castle. This practice, under the bands' Pipe Majors, supervised by the Director of the Army School of Bagpipe Music and Highland Drumming, is doubly useful. It sharpens still further the accuracy of playing and it 'plays in' the pipes, ensuring everyone is tuned to precisely the same pitch.

The Senior Drum Major (McDonald) of The Royal Highland Fusiliers at the rehearsal event that takes place within the castle prior to every performance.

The Pipe Bands tune up for Captain Stuart Samson, Director of Army Bagpipe Music and Highland Drumming.

All this helps to explain the splendid sounds you hear as the massed pipes and drums march out across the drawbridge and down the Esplanade. It is truly something special, well worthy of the Castle setting and in the highest tradition of Army piping.

A musician from The Royal Scots (The Royal Regiment) tests his pipes.

Focusing the sound off the wall helps in tuning the instrument.

The Pipe Major of The Rats of Tobruk tunes a pipe chanter.

A Scots Guard tunes his pipe drones.

Pipers of The Highlanders (above) and
The Rats of Tobruk Memorial Pipes and Drums (below) form circles for final tuning.

A final consultation with Captain Stuart Samson, Director of Army Bagpipe Music and Highland Drumming.

FINAL PREPARATIONS

Two members of the South African
Irish Regiment Pipes and Drums.

A short respite before going on parade.

A snack-break before the big performance.

A member of the Russian
Cossack State Dance Company.

Pipers from The Royal Highland Fusiliers.

Pipers from The Black Watch.

Final uniform adjustments
before going on parade.

Pipers from Scots Guards.

It takes each musician the best
part of an hour to clean and
prepare their uniform, then the
pipers have to spend almost as
long again simply putting it on
ensuring the Tattoo is the finest
display of military bagpipe
music anywhere in the world.

A drummer of The Kings
Own Scottish Borderers.

Drum Major Robson of The Black
Watch (Royal Highland Regiment).

Members of the
motorcycle police
team take time out.

Pipers assemble at the
Castle Gatehouse.

A drummer belonging to the
South African Irish Regiment.

A drummer from the
1st Battalion The Highlanders.

A final chance to buy a
Tattoo programme from
an Edinburgh Boy Scout.

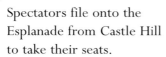

Spectators file onto the
Esplanade from Castle Hill
to take their seats.

Production Team / Lights

Unnoticed by the audience, volunteers operate 12 powerful spotlights around the Esplanade high above the stands. They are accompanied by state of the art computer controlled lights that allow the Esplanade and Castle to be lit in any colour that the Lighting Designer chooses.

Producer Brigadier Melville Jameson, Production Manager Steve Walsh and Major Alasdair Hutton, the Narrator, in the Tattoo Production Box.

THE MAIN EVENT

As the great doors of Edinburgh Castle swing open to reveal some of Scotland's finest soldiers, the cheer from the watching crowd goes up. In immaculate order, the Pipes and Drums march onto the Esplanade, and the night air vibrates to the sound of their music.

Traditionally, this has been the opening sequence of this great show. There follows a string of fast moving displays from some of the most culturally diverse performance Bands & Acts from around the world. These range from music, cultural groups and traditional dancing to exercises of military skill and modern warfare. The colour and the excitement is beyond words.

In the Finale, nobody can fail to be moved by the sound of the Massed Military Bands, when they are joined on the Esplanade by the Massed Pipes and Drums and the power of 500 musicians.

As the evening draws to a close, the Bands are joined by the entire cast and Guard of Honour for the National Anthem, Auld Lang Syne and the Evening Hymn and Sunset.

As the lights dim, the Lone Piper appears on the Castle Ramparts high above the Half-Moon Battery.
The Tattoo concludes as the cast leave the Esplanade, to a cascade of fireworks and the music of "Scotland The Brave".

The programme never fails to thrill. With each subsequent Tattoo, the spectacle moves on a step further. In 2005, images projected onto the castle walls paid tribute to the bi-centenary celebrations of the Battle of Trafalgar and the inspiration provided by Admiral Lord Nelson, who having been shot during the combat, died of his wounds at the moment of his greatest victory.

Astonishingly, the Tattoo has always covered its costs, even with up to 1,000 participants, and such is the international prestige associated with being invited to take part that there has never been a shortage of star attractions. Not that there has ever been a shortage of stars in the audience. Over the years, the Tattoo has played host to British and International Royalty, Hollywood film legends and countless heads of state visiting Scotland.

Times may have changed, but the general public's appetite for pomp and circumstance remains undiminished. The enormous following enjoyed by the Edinburgh Military Tattoo goes to prove that for a large number of people all over the world there is still "something about a soldier."

The Edinburgh Military Tattoo is opened with a fanfare from above the Gatehouse by trumpeters of Her Majesty's Royal Marines.

The Massed Pipes and Drums of thirteen regimental bands march across the drawbridge and onto the Esplanade of Edinburgh Castle.

The Massed Pipes and
Drums as they march
down the Esplanade.

The Massed Pipes and Drums
assembled below the walls of
Edinburgh Castle.

Looking down the Esplanade
from the castle battery.

Pipers of The Royal Scots
(The Royal Regiment) as
they counter-march
on the Esplanade.

Drum Majors of The Royal
Highland Fusiliers (centre),
The Rats of Tobruk Memorial
Pipes and Drums (left) and
The King's Own Scottish
Borderers (right).

The Drum Majors hold
their bands to attention.

The Massed Pipes and Drums form a perfect anchor
to commemorate the bi-centenary celebrations of
Nelson's victory at the Battle of Trafalgar.

Previous page, clockwise from top left, Drum Major of The Royal Gurkha Rifles, Drum Major of The City of Wellington Pipe Band, Drum Major of The South African Irish Pipes and Drums, Band Leader of Her Majesty's Royal Marines, Pipe Major from The Rats of Tobruk Memorial Pipes and Drums, Pipe Major from The City of Wellington Pipe Band, Piper from The Scots Guards and a Drummer from The Argyll and Sutherland Highlanders.

The Band of Her Majesty's Royal Marines (above) and Edinburgh's Kevock Choir (below).

Her Majesty's Royal Marines have a total of five bands. Regarded as the most versatile military musicians in the world, most band members, except solo specialists, are required to attain an acceptable standard on both a string and a wind instrument. The sound and sight of the Corps of Drums precision drill is truly amazing.

Band members of Her Majesty's Royal Marines (above).

A bandsman from The Highland Band of the Scottish Division.

Culture and Colour

The Trinidad and Tobago Defence Force Steel Orchestra was formed in 1995 and are the only marching military steel orchestra in the world.

The Russian Cossack State Dance Company. Dancing is a vital part of Russia's cultural and military heritage. Although the Cossacks were renowned as legendary horsemen and warriors, it was really through their music and dance that they expressed themselves.

Bayonet spinning. His Majesty
The King's Guards Band and
Drill Team of Norway is the
finest unit in the Norwegian
armed forces. Tasked to protect
and serve the Royal Norwegian
Family they also provide
support during forest fires,
search and rescue missions and
for any other national disaster.

The Guardsmen and women
are conscripted under
compulsory military service
for twelve months.

The Cheraw Cultural Dance
Troupe from Mizoram in
the mountain region of
North India.

Dancers accompany The
Military Band of The People's
Liberation Army of China.

A Gombey Dancer
accompanies The Band of the
Bermuda Regiment.

The Traditional Band of the Army of the Republic of Korea.

Performers with the First Royal Band
and Folklore Arts Troupe from Oman.

The US Army Drill Team,
a unit of the 3rd US Infantry
go through their paces with
razor sharp bayonets.

Dynamic drumming by the
Top Secret Drum Corps
from Switzerland.

An Aboriginal dancer leaps into the air as part of Australia's Anarungga Dance Company.

The Cook Island National Youth Dance Team from the South Pacific.

The Imps performance
includes a series of high speed
combination 'cross overs', a five
bike sixteen strong rolling
pyramid and a two car jump.

A perfected mini pyramid by the
younger members of the Imps
Motor Cycle Display Team.

Originating in the 1970's
The Imps Motor Cycle Display
Team is a charity for deprived
children founded by Roy Pratt
MBE. The thirty eight young
riders are aged between five
and sixteen.

Although there have
been Highland Dancers
performing since the very
first Tattoo, the Edinburgh
Tattoo Highland Dancers
was established in 1995.
Here they have combined
with The New Zealand
Highland Dancers to form
a one hundred-strong
dance troupe.

The Band and Bugles of The Light Division were formed in 1994 from bands of The Light Infantry and The Royal Green Jackets. Upholding traditions going back to the Napoleonic Wars, the bugle replaced the drum as the means of communication on the battlefield. They are able to react quickly and can march at the double time of 140 paces per minute.

Her Majesty's Royal Marine Commandos comprise a highly-trained, high-readiness, light amphibious expeditionary function, capable of surgical strikes from the sea.

As the sun sets the early evening Saturday performance draws to a close.

2005 saw the first image projections. Here Admiral Lord Nelsons' flagship the Victory is projected onto the walls of Edinburgh Castle.

The Massed Military
Bands accompanied by
The Kevock Choir.

The fireworks commence as the
Massed Pipes and Drums join
the Massed Military Bands.

The full cast of over 1000 fill the Esplanade for the Finale and the National Anthem.

The cast are allowed to
"about turn" to enjoy the
firework display over the
Castle on Saturday evenings.

Standing on a small platform atop the ramparts of the Half-Moon Battery, exposed to any weather and with a sheer drop to Johnston Terrace below, the famous Lone Piper plays 'Lest We Forget' to end the Edinburgh Military Tattoo. Nowadays, the 'honour' is rotated amongst senior pipers from the various Pipes and Drums participating at the Tattoo.

The piper is required to put on a safety harness just in case.

The Massed Pipes and
Drums march down Castle
Hill to Scotland The Brave.

Next page - All over
and time to relax.

Taking warmth from the
Saltire, The National Flag
of Scotland.

A final salute from 7 year old Jordan Becker (Imp).

It takes some nerve for the Producer with a massive cast
from home and overseas to 'get the show on the road'
with just three days rehearsal – a challenge indeed.

However, the Edinburgh Tattoo, both on the Esplanade
and behind the scene, runs with traditional military
precision and provides, for the millions who see it, a
memorable spectacle – once seen, never forgotten.

A final gathering of Pipe and Drum Majors together with the
Director of Army Bagpipe Music & Highland Drumming on the
steps of the War Memorial, Edinburgh Castle.

The
EDINBURGH
Military
TATTOO

1969